Hi, I'm Sarah.

And your name is...? _____

Jennifer Moore-Mallinos / Marta Fàbrega

It's Called
Dyslexia

sourcebooks
eXplore

LEARNING HOW TO READ AND WRITE

I'm so excited! I'm going to learn how to read and write this year at school. How hard can it be? In fact, I think it's going to be so much fun! There are so many books I want to explore, especially the ones about dinosaurs. I can't wait!

So far, I can remember some of the letters and sounds in the alphabet. Except I keep mixing up the letters "b" and "d" and the sounds "f" and "v." Because of that, the hardest part is sounding out words. It's very confusing! I get all mixed up and just want to give up. But then I think about all of those dinosaur books I want to read, so I keep trying.

SOUNDING OUT WORDS

I FEEL SAD

Every day I still have trouble sounding out
the words, especially the beginning part.
I even find it hard to remember the names
of certain things. Sometimes I feel so sad
that I pretend I'm sick so I don't have
to go to school. Why is reading so easy for
the rest of the class, but so hard for me?

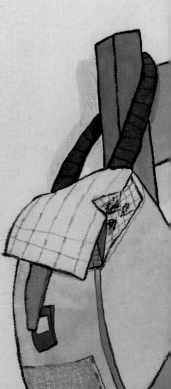

I WORK REALLY HARD IN CLASS

I like going to school and seeing my friends. I work really hard in class, but yesterday when my teacher stopped by my desk, I got scared. She said that she noticed that when we sang the alphabet, I was having trouble remembering the right order of the letters. My teacher thought it would be a good idea to talk to Mom and Dad.

WHY CAN'T I READ AND WRITE WELL?

At the meeting, my teacher told my parents that I was having trouble with my reading and writing. My teacher said that she wanted me to do some special tests. Maybe there was a reason why I was having so much trouble learning to read and write.

I HAVE DYSLEXIA, BUT I'LL IMPROVE

The tests that I took were actually fun.
We sang nursery rhymes, we played
a matching game of rhyming words,
and we clapped along to the syllables of
different words. When the tests were over,
the teacher looked at how I had done.
She told me and my mom and dad that
I had something called dyslexia.

IT JUST TAKES ME A BIT LONGER

At first I was scared. But when my teacher
explained that having dyslexia meant that it
would just take me longer to learn how to read
and write, I didn't feel so bad. It didn't mean
that I wasn't smart, and it didn't mean that
I couldn't be good at other things. It just meant
that I would need a little extra help and a lot
of hard work.

PLENTY OF HELP AT SCHOOL AND AT HOME

I found out that I wasn't the only person to have dyslexia. There are other kids in my school who also need extra help. My teacher uses special programs that improve our listening, reading, and writing skills. My favorite is when we use the color coded tiles or the picture and word cue cards. They really help!

MY READING IS
IMPROVING

It took a lot of practice and hard work, but my reading's getting better and I don't feel so sad anymore. I haven't pretended to be sick in a long time. And I've read five of the dinosaur books I wanted to read. My teacher and parents have been showing me fun ways to remember words and patterns. I have also learned some tricks to help me pay attention better. And now, learning is finally getting a little easier.

POETRY IS AWESOME!

Today my teacher read some funny rhyming poems to the class. I was excited when my teacher asked us to make our very own book of poems. Because now that I'm getting better with my words, I was able to write some poems.
I couldn't wait to show the teacher and my parents all of my silly poems!

IT'S NOT AS CONFUSING AS IT USED TO BE

Even though I had to use my picture dictionary to help me spell some of the words for my poems, I didn't get as confused as before. And using my computer to type my poems helped, too. I didn't have to worry about my handwriting and correcting my mistakes was easier. It took a few days to finish, but I did it!

At the beginning of the school year my teacher let me practice Whisper Reading with a partner because I was too scared to read out loud to the class. But not anymore! I couldn't wait for my turn to read some of my poems. I wasn't nervous at all, and I wasn't worried about making mistakes either.

I READ IN FRONT OF THE ENTIRE CLASS!

IT WAS SO AWESOME!

After I read a couple of my poems out loud to my class, everybody stood up and clapped. They really liked them! My teacher said that my poem about dinosaurs, that one called "Tex the Rex," won the special prize for the best poem!

I HAVE DYSLEXIA, AND THAT'S OK

I have dyslexia and that's OK! I might have to work harder and practice longer to learn how to read and write, but it's worth it! I feel so much better about myself, especially now that I learned I have a talent for writing poetry! Maybe one day I'll be famous like Albert Einstein, Leonardo da Vinci, Walt Disney, Beethoven, Muhammad Ali, Steven Spielberg, and Bill Gates! They all have dyslexia, too!

Activities

WHISPER READING

Whisper Reading is a technique used to practice getting used to reading out loud.

1. Choose a book that you are already familiar with.
2. Practice reading the book silently by yourself.
3. Practice reading the book in a whisper by yourself.
4. Choose a partner (family member, teacher, or friend) and whisper read a few pages, or whisper read the WHOLE book if you are ready.

Then before you know it, reading out loud won't be so hard or scary!

WHISPER READING "PHONES"

A fun way to practice Whisper Reading is by whispering into a "phone."

1. A "phone" can be made out of a toilet paper or gift wrap roll.
2. Don't forget to decorate your "phone." Be creative and have some fun!

Using a "phone" will help make your voice louder, which makes it easy to hear the sounds and words more clearly.

LET'S BAKE OR COOK!

Baking and cooking are fun, interactive activities that not only end with a treat, but also involve reading.

Reading recipes so you can create something yummy for you and your family is such a nice thing to do. And it also reminds you how important reading really is!

With the help of an adult, follow the instructions, measure the ingredients, and cook away! Enjoy!

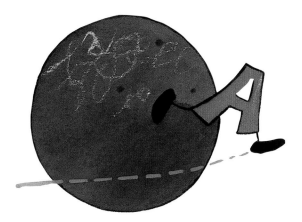

LETTER ART

We learn when we are having fun. And it's even better when the learning activity uses any of the five senses.

So let's have some fun while we're learning letters and sounds.

1. Choose the material that you would like to practice writing your letters in, like shaving cream, sand, water, or putty.
2. If you choose shaving cream or sand, simply spread the product out evenly over a flat surface. (You may want to use a cookie sheet or tray in order to help prevent a mess.) Start practicing your letters. When done, simply "erase" the letter and try again.
3. Water is fun to use outside on the sidewalk or on a wall with a paintbrush.
4. If you're using putty, simply roll the putty out into strips and design your letters. When done, roll it all back together and start all over again.
5. Don't forget to say the letter and make the sound.

MATCHING BOWL OF RHYMES

Games that involve rhyming can help build decoding skills.

When we use our knowledge of the relationship between letters and sounds to correctly sound out words, we are decoding. This includes knowing not only the sound of letters but also the sound of the letter patterns that we see in many words, such as "-tion."

1. Fill a bowl with objects.
2. Each object must have another object in the bowl that rhymes with it. For example, a "dog" figurine and a picture of a "log," or a picture of a "cat" and a "bat" figurine.
3. Each player takes a turn picking an object out of the bowl.
4. The next player has to find the object in the bowl that rhymes with it.
5. Players take turns finding the rhyming objects.

Parent's guide

All parents want their children to be successful. We want them to be happy and to succeed in school and in life. We want our children to grow up to be confident adults who can contribute and thrive within society in a meaningful way. So, how do we as parents make this happen? What can we do to help our children to have a satisfying future? How do we help them to become successful learners?

The stepping-stones toward learning start with the most basic skills: reading, writing, and mathematics. These basic skills are the foundation on which knowledge is built. Therefore, there are high expectations placed on these primary skills for every child to master within a relatively short period of time. However, not all children will grasp these concepts as quickly as we would like, and some will require additional support to do so.

Children who struggle in any area of academics whether it's reading, writing, or math, often experience stress and frustration. This will ultimately develop into a reluctance to go to school as well as a display of negative behaviors, such as uncooperativeness, defiance, and even depression and withdrawal. These behaviors, in combination with poor achievement, may indicate an even greater problem that will require further exploration in order to identify the core issue.

A child who is having difficulty learning how to read and write or who is struggling to master certain skills will show a repeated pattern of mistakes.

Approximately 10 to 15 percent of the population is dyslexic, but many of these people are not identified in early childhood. Although there are almost an equal number of boys and girls affected, boys tend to show their symptoms much earlier than girls do. The symptoms of dyslexia indicate a problem with auditory processing, that is, the ability to recognize, analyze, segment, and blend sounds. People affected often have difficulty processing and understanding what they hear, especially when attempting to learn the connection between letters and sounds. They may have problems comprehending rapid instructions or following more than one command at a time. Difficulty with reading emerges early on, when children fail to see and hear similarities and differences in letters and sounds and therefore can't assemble the parts of words.

One of the common signs of dyslexia is reversals. Reversals occur when a person confuses letters by either reading or writing letters incorrectly, such as "b" and "d," or when a word order is reversed, such as "rats" read as "star" or "not" read as "ton."

Subsequent spelling, writing, and handwriting difficulties often result. Mathematics skills may also be affected when a child can't remember math facts. The symptoms of dyslexia vary from individual to individual, but in-depth evaluation can highlight both strengths and weaknesses.

In the classroom, the struggle with decoding often makes it difficult for children to comprehend reading matter as well as to convey their thoughts on paper. As a result, they may feel frustrated, embarrassed, and discouraged, and do whatever they can to avoid reading and writing. In many cases, "bad" behavior will become the distraction or way out of having to address their difficulties.

Unfortunately, when children experience failure on a regular basis, they will also experience low self-esteem and sometimes describe themselves as "stupid." For this reason, it is very important that parents and educators attempt to increase a child's confidence level through consistent praise and support.

As mentioned in the story, it may also be beneficial to find an activity in which the child does well. This will help him or her with confidence and the positive feelings associated with success.

A child diagnosed with dyslexia does not lack intelligence, potential, or the ability to become a successful and confident member of society. In fact, there are many famous people who were diagnosed with dyslexia. Some had to struggle without special help and others learned to adapt to their diagnosis. Despite their difficulties, they were able to make valuable contributions to society.

Parents are the most important advocates for their children. Be aware, at all times, that specialized instruction, one-to-one tutorial, and plenty of determination and positive support will make the difference. Every child with dyslexia can be successful!

First published in the United States in 2009 by BES and Gemser Publications.

Copyright © Gemser Publications, S.L, 2022
c/ Castell, 38; Teià 08329 (Barcelona) – Spain (World Rights)
Website: www.gemserpublications.com
E-mail: merce@mercedesros.com
Illustrator: Marta Fàbrega
Author: Jennifer Moore-Mallinos

Published by Sourcebooks eXplore, an imprint of Sourcebooks
P.O. Box 4410, Naperville, Illinois 60567-4410
(630) 961-3900
sourcebookskids.com

Cataloging-in-Publication Data is on file with the Library of Congress.

Source of Production: HeShan Astros Printing Ltd. Industrial Development Area Xijiang River, Gulao Town, HeShan, GuangDong, China.
Date of Production: May 2024
Run Number:5040271

Printed and bound in China.
LEO 10 9 8 7 6 5 4 3 2